CAMBRIDGE LIBRARY COLLECTION

Books of enduring scholarly value

Travel and Exploration

The history of travel writing dates back to the Bible, Caesar, the Vikings and the Crusaders, and its many themes include war, trade, science and recreation. Explorers from Columbus to Cook charted lands not previously visited by Western travellers, and were followed by merchants, missionaries, and colonists, who wrote accounts of their experiences. The development of steam power in the nineteenth century provided opportunities for increasing numbers of 'ordinary' people to travel further, more economically, and more safely, and resulted in great enthusiasm for travel writing among the reading public. Works included in this series range from first-hand descriptions of previously unrecorded places, to literary accounts of the strange habits of foreigners, to examples of the burgeoning numbers of guidebooks produced to satisfy the needs of a new kind of traveller - the tourist.

My Diary in a Chinese Farm

Published in Tokyo in 1894, Mrs Archibald Little's diary of her summer stay at a local farmhouse in the Chinese interior near Chongqing provides a first-hand account of rural Chinese life in the nineteenth century from a European's perspective. Little was an accomplished author, having written numerous novels on women's social roles under her maiden name, Bewicke. In *My Diary*, she continues this theme of women's place in society. Her account also touches on the interactions between Christian missionaries and the local people. She was an active campaigner against the Chinese tradition of binding the feet of young girls, and helped to bring about its abolition. A limited run of only 500 copies of *My Diary* was originally printed. It contains 26 illustrations and is an invaluable historical source for studying rural life in nineteenth-century China.

My Diary in a Chinese Farm

Alicia E. Neva Little

CAMBRIDGE UNIVERSITY PRESS

Cambridge, New York, Melbourne, Madrid, Cape Town, Singapore,
São Paolo, Delhi, Dubai, Tokyo

Published in the United States of America by Cambridge University Press, New York

www.cambridge.org
Information on this title: www.cambridge.org/9781108013833

This edition first published 1898
This digitally printed version 2010

ISBN 978-1-108-01383-3 Paperback

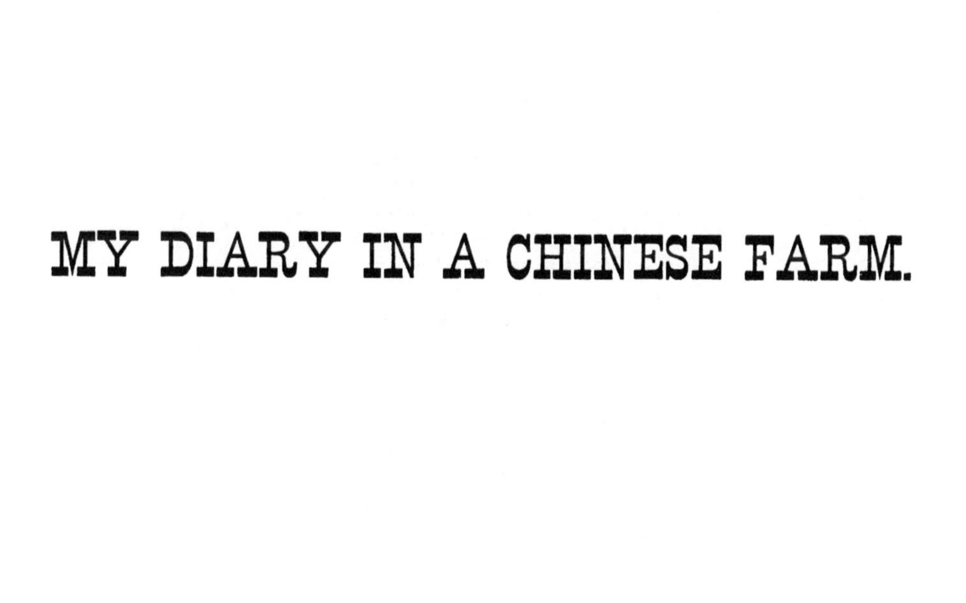

MY DIARY IN A CHINESE FARM.

MY DIARY

IN

A CHINESE FARM

BY

Mrs. ARCHIBALD LITTLE

(A. E. N. BEWICKE).

"I DESIRE TO PRODUCE IN MYSELF A LOVING HEART TOWARDS ALL LIVING CREATURES."

"IF THOU BE BORN IN THE POOR MAN'S HOVEL, YET HAVE WISDOM, THEN WILT THOU BE LIKE THE LOTUS-FLOWER GROWING OUT OF THE MIRE."

KELLY & WALSH, LIMITED,

SHANGHAI, HONGKONG, SINGAPORE & YOKOHAMA.

COLLOTYPES AND PHOTO-ENGRAVINGS

BY

K. OGAWA,

Tokyo, Japan.

INTRODUCTORY WORDS.

We were living in the far West of China, 1500 miles from the sea, 500 miles beyond the reach of steamers, and against its becoming too hot in Chung-king, a large city, the commercial Capital of Szechuan, all shut in by walls, and so full of houses as not to have an available breathing space left empty, we had rented a hill side on which to build ourselves a Summer cottage. But the Magistrate had stopped our building on the pretext that the country people were so much opposed to foreigners he dared not sanction our living amongst them ; then made a great favour of having persuaded a certain Farmer to have us as tenants, and suggested that, if we went out to him for three months, perhaps gradually the people might become accustomed to us.

It was very hot in the daytime and all day long I was shut up in the one Farm house sittingroom, so I started a Diary for much the same reason probably, that I have often observed people do so on a Sea Voyage. They generally do not keep it up till the end, neither did I; but I noted down every thing I could observe of interest, as long as I wrote in it, and here it is, recalling many simple pleasures and some painful days.

"Sorrow and Shine is Life, little Annie, Flower and Thorn."

Country House on the Yangtse.

MY DIARY IN A CHINESE FARM.

JULY 6th, 1893. After all I went off to the Farm by myself, starting at ten, and only getting there after twelve, though the crossing of the River was rather exciting than slow, there being no freshet on; only all the dreadful rocks, that went to form the remarkable little harbour of the Dragon's gate, were now quite covered with water, so that our boat went careering over them. Yet afterwards it was so hot, that the coolies spent a long time eating and resting before they got me up the 1000 ft. from the River to the T'u Shan Temple, on the top of the first range of hills. I was annoyed to find the furniture in our Farm not cleaned, and a good deal of smell of dirt in spite of the many men, who had been out cleaning it for several days. The Shrine at one end of the room, that I had told the people they might take away, was still there. When I remarked on this, the Cook exclaimed it could not be moved. "Well then it must be cleaned," I said, attacking it with a feather brush, and immediately producing a shower of dust. The Coolies all screamed. "You must not touch it! We cannot touch it!" they cried. "Call the woman of the house," I said. But she again waved deprecatory hands, and cried "I cannot touch it," to which the Coolies all replied in Chorus: "She cannot touch it! A ***woman!***" Presently the Farmer appeared, very obliging but very grave. It seemed that he only could clean it. But he proceeded to do so with so much reverence, it was evident the accumulations of dust would never get removed. So I rubbed, and brushed, and generally knocked things about, for other people to put together, till gradually the whole erection came somewhat to pieces amidst showers of dirt. "The ***Pusa*** (Image) cannot like dirt," I continued to repeat. But at last they managed to convey to me, that it was not a Shrine with a ***Pusa,*** but the Holy Place, where the Ancestral Tablets were kept. "Oh the Ancestors!" I then said. "Well they do not like dirt. They like to be clean," on which both the Farmer and his wife seemed greatly amused, especially the latter, who quite agreed, but would not touch anything. "We put fresh flowers before the pictures of ***our*** Ancestors," I said. On which the children brandished crackers in my face, to show what a much better way they had of honouring their dead. Meanwhile the Farmer and the eldest son cleaned the Tablet, the vase containing Incense Sticks etc., etc., and I was delighted to find one Coolie could now really clean the outside of the Shrine, and all the particularly dirty boards on the top. Whilst no one objected to my taking all the musty books out of the Cupboard underneath, drying them in the sun, dusting them, and then putting them away tidily in the end. The eldest son then tore off the old red paper strips, and proceeded to write on new red papers "As still with us, though above," which was stuck up above the Ancestral tablet, a little looking glass being very carefully hung in the middle. I pleaded to have it washed first. After all this great display of reverence what was my surprise to find that we were now quite at liberty to place our stores in the cupboard underneath! And our Boy with perfect calm stood two commanding looking bottles on the top right in front of the ancestral tablet. Nor did anyone seem to see anything amiss in the arrangement.

They are busy weaving their Cotton, and we fell asleep to the sound of the Loom in the next room, and heard it already going on again, when we awoke next morning.

July 7th. Wore my Chinese clothes for the first time, found them delightfully cool, and decided I would wear nothing else till the hot weather was over. A very trying day! Thunderstorms, and not a breath of air even on the top of our hill in the second and higher Range, 1300 ft. above the River, 2000 ft. above the sea.

July 8th. They were busy spinning Yarn at the Farm to-day, and all the concrete, Threshing floor outside our windows, that makes such a good place to sit out on in the moonlight, was taken up with their Yarn stretched on long frames. Found the cotton bandages, I wore last year with straw sandals, were not comfortable, so the Farmer's wife offered to bind my feet for me. She did so just like her own poor little stunted things, only using broader bandages, about 2½ yards long, as my 2 feet were so much bigger, and to my surprise her way of binding the feet was not only tidy but most comfortable, supporting the foot, just where it needs support.

Went up the hill, then seeing a great thunderstorm coming on across the hundred miles or so of country we see from there in all directions, I hurried down and sat outside without changing, watching the rain advance. Alas! I had on my cool Chinese clothes offering no protection against the change in the weather, so caught a severe chill round my waist, and felt no energy to go with the Farmer's wife, who was most eager and excited about it, to see what had happened, when there was a sharp clap like the sudden report of a gun—just over our heads, without any following roll, and something fell in a Paddy field below. A crowd of people collected, and we heard afterwards, there was a strong smell of sulphur and saw the stone corner of a wayside Shrine which was knocked off, but whatever fell got lost in the soft Paddy field.

July 9th. High fever all night, and aches in all my bones! was carried back to town in the evening through the rain, A. sturdily marching along in Pyjamas, raised very high, though not quite as high as the Coolies, who displayed their very well shaped legs pretty well in their entirety. I was carefully dressed en Européenne once more. It is certainly much more convenient, as well as far more becoming.

July 18th. Started before 6 A. M. for the Farm, but took so long crossing the river, did not get there till after 12, and I felt the sun very much. Air there fresh and fragrant, reminding one of hay-making days.

July 19th. Mistress of the Farm flogged little Grandson, because he had a sore on his leg, and had not washed it properly. She does her washing of clothes in the most delightful fashion in a large wooden tray, brought out and stood on forms under the fine Walnut tree, that shades our threshing floor. She washes clothes beautifully clean, although using no soap. To-day they are sizing the Yarn with rice-water, drying it, after boiling, in the very powerful sun. As we wanted a stable for our pony, and also disliked the

Our Farm.

smell of the Mao Sze and pig sty, the latter as a rule in Szechuan placed under the former, they are cading the old one to us for a Stable, and have built themselves a new one. It is quite palatial, much the most carefully plastered place about the Farm. It is of course the source of all the fertility we see around us.

The eldest daughter came out to spend the day. She arrived in a Chair with a sad tale. Her husband had beaten her. He keeps a small shop for selling clothes-stuffs, and, as far as I could make out, she had ordered new clothes of a tailor without insisting that the material should be out of her husband's shop. When the bill came he refused to pay, but beat her instead. We took Poney and Chair on to hills behind but, though we went after five, the sun's slanting rays made me feel so sick, that we just lay still on the shady side of the hill, and gazed at the view—particularly clear, bathed in sunshine as it was, although we looked at it from the shade of our Limestome Range. The high mountain in the distance, round which I had so often seen the thunderstorms gather, and which now stands out quite clear with table top, and several rows of precipices, shining white in the sunshine, turns out to be the Chin Fo Shan, Golden Buddha Mountain, six days journey off, and to which two sets of Missionaries have just gone seeking for a Sanitarium. One of our Coolies, who has been a Soldier, says he went there with his General to burn Incense, but when he was there the accommodation in the Temple on the top was much too bad to stop there. He says there are Chinese there, but that there is also a tribe of Miaotse (Aborigines) and that it is on the borders of the Province of Kweichow. The country people all cluster round to talk to our men, and seem greatly interested to tell about one set of Missionaries, who had got a small child with them and five Coolies carrying loads, nine people in all. We hope they will find a shelter, and hear that the Inns along the way are good, but that it is a hot journey, as indeed it looks.

In the evening we were just falling asleep, sitting outside in the moonlight, enjoying the most refreshing breeze, when one of the boys came up to A. again to ask, when he would bring out his foreign gun. The boy had displayed the greatest interest in this gun all day long. And presently it appeared all the men of the Farm were going out with heavy sticks, and rough spears to hunt an animal—what we could not make out—that stole their Indian Corn. So we went too, Cook and Coolies and all. We climbed up and up to the very top of the cultivated ground. And there the men proceeded to dig. They had stopped up one burrow by day with stones and earth, but they said there were three. As the digging went on, another man appeared with one of our candles—given by the Cook for the occasion—and which being European guttered shockingly in the breeze. Then the two dogs found us out, and great was our alarm, lest the long haired Terrier should be taken in the flickering light and shadow for the animal we had all come out to kill, and pressing were the men's entreaties to our beautiful black Pointer to come and point out the wild beast, or as they said dig for it. But Beau refused to be in the least interested, and rightly so, for it seemed what we had all come out to hunt was a Wild Boar, and now it appeared he emphatically was not at home as our Coolies dug and dug, and poked their spears into where his nose should have appeared. So the peaceful beauty of the moonless sky with its galaxy of stars, and landscape looking perfectly lovely, now that the somewhat ugly foreground of Paddy fields was veiled by night, was unsullied. We found the air much fresher up there, and tried to call the stars by their names, then came all stumbling down the steep hill side again. The Mistress of the Farm regretted much she had not been able to go too, but when all the men go out somebody must stop at home she said. It seems now that this very well to do Farm, where they are always pressing roasted cobs of Indian Corn upon us, does not posses even one Chinese candle, their artificial illumination being confined to the flame of a pith wick in a saucer of pea oil.

July 20th. The beautiful Tiger-lily the Farm children brought in with such pride about a fortnight ago, saying its buds would open in water, and coming each morning to boast over them, is over now. So is an orange and cream Lily they brought in the day before yesterday, and that at once made the Tiger lily look quite faded. The strange looking scarlet flower, that I only know as the Dragon boat flower, has now shrivelled up. The Cook tells us after all he is not going to marry a Szechuan woman. We thought it was all arranged, and had lent him money for the wedding festivities. He says now, as soon as we can spare him he wants to go home for a time to his own Province of Hupeh. For, as he says, all the women here smoke Tobacco, and many smoke opium, and how can you know beforehand? It is true they are cheap. You can get a wife for 10 Taels (about £ 1. 10s) or a very good one for 20 Taels. But then suppose you had paid your money, and found out in the end she smoked, there you would be with your 20 Taels gone! Now in Hupeh he could know all about the parentage and connections of the girl he should choose. Wise man! evidently convinced of the truth of heredity without a Galton to teach him. But what odd people the Chinese are! The head of the Counting House tells A. "I have sent word down River never to insure Shrimps again. It is a dreadful cargo. You see it smells, and then the Porpoises and all the other big fishes find out what it is and make a disturbance in the water trying to get in to rescue their brethren in Captivity." Even the Roman Catholic Clerk says "There must be myriads of souls in that cargo of Shrimps that has been wrecked." Went for a delightful walk along the hills to the South, walking along their shady side among the Fir trees. A little bird flow from almost under my feet, and I found its nest between four tall stalks, with four spotted eggs; begged the Coolies not to touch it and had the satisfaction on passing an hour later of seeing the same little birdy fly out. A lovely green Praying Mantis came into our room to-day. But the moon was watery at night, and few stars visible. It looks as if it were working up for another storm. A very hot day, though the thermometer in the Farm did not rise above 86., bat then its lofty room with thick, thatched roof keeps out a good deal of heat.

July 21st. Several visitors to-day, one a married daughter of the Farm with a very cross, little doy of three, not yet weaned, and chiefly dressed in a pinafore worked all over back and front in cross stitch by his mother. The other a young woman, elaborately rouged, with pink nails, her hair brushed in two strands, one to the right, the other to the left across the forehead, thus crossing in the middle of it, and shewing no parting, a singularly disfiguring fashion. She had white flowers in a wreath all round her back hair. A pair of white cotton trousers with blue cetton borders, and

Family Group.

a rather long white jucket similary trimmed completed her toilette. She was too smart to do much. But the daughter of the house immediately set to work to help her mother in getting out of a sort of nettle the fibre used for making grass cloth, and worked at this pretty well all day, when not suckling her child. The breaking the stalks without breaking the outside skin made the peeling this skin off seem to require some knack, and I did not try it. But I found it easy enough to strip the fibre from the skin, when I had the proper implements. Taking a thing like a small iron spud with sharp edges in the right hand, and inserting the thumb of the right hand into a roll, that just about filled up the spud, when placed inside it, one then takes the skin of the tall nettle in the left hand, and draws it again and again between the sharp spud, and the thumb covering, till the fibres are quite clean. The sky was overcast, so that it was quite pleasant sitting outside, but the Mistress of the Farm would not allow me to become an adept, shewing me her hands all stained with the nettle, and requesting me to keep my dress carefully clear of it, for fear that should get stained too. Then they all talked about me in their local Chinese, saying to one another 'She does not understand!' which alas! was true. Presently a man came round with two baskets dangling from his pole all full of pop corn, some of it made up into cakes with molasses, but most of it in parcels. No one shewed any eagerness to buy, not even the children. I tasted one of the cakes, and then presented it to one of the children, telling our Boy to buy some for the others. But this which seemed so natural to me was an unintelligible idea to them and they all began to buy for themselves, and presently were all munching. There was some complaint about the price, when the Seller said it was a long way to bring the cakes from Chungking, so my idea that they looked so clean, because made in some clean healthy Farm house near by, fell through.

In the afternoon I rode our Poney to the top of the hill, and then told the old man, whom we have engaged to take charge of him while here to lead him away to meet A. But the Poney took charge, leading the old man a perfect dance all over the mountain top after nice patches of grass, indulging in rolls between whiles, saddle and all. The old man talked to him a great deal. But in the end I had to exert myself, or they never would have got down the hill at all. They had hardly been gone half an hour, before there was a merry neighing, and there appeared round the mountain side a most gaily caparisoned Poney with high red, Chinese saddle, a whole collar of large bells, and a very large red tassel hanging down over his neck. A man led him, and a man followed him, and presently appeared the young man from the grand house, whose large garden is the landmark we coast round to arrive at our Farm. He walked along, fanning himself, but at once made for me to ask endless questions as to whether we would sell our Poney, our foreign saddle, our dogs, whether we would buy his Poney, and when we would go again to his house to "***Shwa***" that most expressive Chungking word for ***generally enjoy oneself.*** His great delight was again and again to ask me if I would sell our long haired Terrier, Jack, what the Chinese call a Lion Dog, because I always definitely answered I would not. But appearently what he really wanted was the foreign saddle. He said he had given 50 Taels (about £ 8) for his Poney, which was from

Chungking from across the Yangtse.

Kweichow, and wanted to know what we wanted for ours. At last the sun was so near setting he thought it prudent to go away, as he said it was sure to rain directly the sun went down. But instead of that it turned into a lovely, clear night again. It appears now the Weavers in the next room are only tenants at the Farm like ourselves. They were working later than ever last night.—It is very tiresome, as we cannot sleep for their weaving. They never leave off. I shall be curious to know what rent they pay. We pay by arrangement of the Magistrate £6 for our two rooms for three months—ten times as much as a Chinese family would pay for the same accommodation. We gave up one room however, to which we were entitled, the Farm people declaring they with their large family must move out, if we used it, and now we find they were all the time letting this other room.

July 22nd. To-day was a difficult day to get through, for A. had invited to dinner the 16 Elders of the neighbouring Districts, who had called on him before we moved out, bringing a large red card with all their names upon it, and a congratulation upon our change of residence. And as they just filled two tables leaving no room for him and his Comprador, he had invited 6 Chungking men to fill the third table. The best dinner Chungking could provide had been ordered, at a charge of 4,000 Cash (at present exchange about 10s.) per table of 8 people, including use of crockery. Our men began coming over from the City quite early; they decided it was impossible for 24 people to dine in our sitting-room, two tables must be set outside notwithstanding the Sun, so sent back to Chungking for our

Courtyard awning to hang from the Walnut tree outside. This did not arrive till about one, and the City guests began arriving at eleven. First came the Banker in a long gown of white silk with a sort of little gauze stripe in it. When he took this off, as they all did to eat, he appeared in a short Jacket of stiff black gauze with a grey stripe. The Comprador was in a long gown of grey Pongee silk. The Literary Man, and A. in white grasscloth gowns. The Elders almost all had short coats, but one or two had new long gowns for the occasion, and all had very smart silk over-trousers. They looked a most respectable set of men. They insisted upon the City men sitting inside, as it was cooler, and they said they were all Country people, accustomed to sit out of doors. And the City gentlemen sent me a request to sit down and dine with them, as there was a slight difficulty about my being served in my bedroom. However I declined, as I thought they might like to strip to the waist, as Chinese usually do in Summer. But it being in the country they found it so much cooler, they did not in the end care to do so. I think dinner began about two and at last I got some dishes brought me, which seemed very good. After dinner I took two Photographs of the party, which seemed greatly to delight the Elders. And they took leave apparently in a most enthusiastic state of mind, thanking profusely. The City men went away together at a quarter to five. We then went to the top of our hill, sitting as usual by the foundations of our unfinished house. I rode up on an English side saddle, and found it much more tiring than astride. Presently appeared the smart Poney, and

Dinner Party to Village Elders.

the young man from the grand house, with all his retinue. A. after a while took him back to our Farm, for tea. It seems he is 17, and reading for his Bachelor's Examination. He looks much more like 24, and is already married. He begged us to go and *Shwa* at their house next day. The family consists of the Widows and Sons of a wealthy retired Official.

After the dinner was over, all our Coolies, and the Chair-coolies of the guests sat down at once to what remained. The women of the Farm had a table to themselves, and also their portion of the feast, with which they seemed dilighted. After they had all finished one of our Coolies was very eager for me to satisfy myself, that on wine was left in the large Jar, that had been brought out. This I quite believd. But the tone in which he said, it had been excellent, was worth hearing. The feast was inaugurated by about five minutes of Crackers, which had been hung in long garlands from the trees, where they looked quite pretty,—like strings of red Peppers, till they began to sputter and go off. We had laid in a good stock, and besides this the Banker brought out another supply as a present. I understand that in accordance with custom we presented 100 Cash (about 3d.) to the Chair coolies of each of our guests, who came in a Chair. What they gave to our Servant I do not know. However all the Twansheo Elders walked, and to the Head man among them we were indebted for the loan of extra tables, and benches. Our farmer is one of the Twansheo. We played Chess by moonlight in the evening to the great delight of the Farm people, who could not however understand all our pieces being able to cross the River i.e. the middle of the board, as only some of their pieces can. Then A. had Mosquito curtains hung from the Walnut tree, and slept on a Travelling bed outside.

Noticed to-day the little Grange tree in front of the house is covered with very large green Oranges, and the Pomegranate tree beside it has also many fruits. They have picked off the vine so many stone-hard grapes, which they were greatly disappointed at my being unable to eat in that condition, that I fear none remain to ripen. The children have brought me fresh, huge bunches of the scarlet Dragon Flower. It turns out it is called Dragon's claws, not Dragon boat, from the flowers likeness to claws. It is all brilliant scarlet, Calyx, Corolla, stalk and all, and looks very well mixed with Ferns and grasses.

Hoang Ko Tree.

To-day is the beginning of great heat, according to the Chinese Calender, but the Thermometer was between 78 and 81 all day here, and there was generally a light brerze.

July 23rd. We took the little Poney, and went along the hills to the south, a delightful shady path. Then A. insisted on going down the Steep mountain road, all stone steps, to see the Wayside Inn, that had so taken my fancy from a distance. It is very prettily situated with two grand Hoang Ko trees (Ficus Infectoria), a kind of Banyan, very shady in front of the door, and looking on to tree clad hills with breezy slopes rising behind, and a very fine little breeze of its own coming up the valley. But its surroundings were so dirty and neglected it seemed useless to recommend it to Chung-king friends needing a change. There were two tolerable sized rooms thrown into one, full of straw mattressed beds and nothing else, rather dark, looking on to a dirty Courtyard; of course infinitely better than the accommodation we often get in travelling, but still hardly what one would leave one's own 'house for even for a night. We both slept under Walnut tree, but there was no breeze, and the dogs barked horribly.

July 24th. A. got into his Office by 6 A.M. to-day. After he had left I dressed and went for a delightful walk getting back by 6-30. I went towards the Fortress of Refuge on the top of the highest mountain in the neighbourhood, 2500 ft. above the sea, that is such a striking object in all the views all round, its battlements connecting the two tops of the hill, finally linked by the gateway, through which to-day I saw the sun rising. The air was 'so fresh, and the scene in its wildness so reminded me ef Cumberland Moors I wondered why one complained of the Summer here. But the Thermometer only varied from 80-86 in the 24 hrs., and after a whole number of women had come flocking in to see me, inviting one another to sit down, looking into my bedroom, and generally making themselves quite at home, and ignoring my feelings, I only felt equal to being carried up the hill in the evening, and sitting in the Chair to enjoy the breeze. There was distant thunder. And it looked so like a storm, and seemed so defenceless to sleep outside by myself I did not at all want to. But there were the Mosquito curtains, and the Cook began preparing my bed under-

Fortress of Refuge.

neath as a matter of course. So I was ashamed to say I was afraid, the more so as there were the three dogs to give me good warning if anyone come near. When I went out to get into bed there was our soldier coolie, not only stretched at full length in one of our Mountain Chairs, but having established it alongside of my bed. "What are you doing there?" I asked "This is my bed," he replied. "I always sleep in this Chair." "Why is it not in its usual place?" "There are so many Mosquitoes under the eaves!" he replied with cool effrontery. "Dreadful lot of Mosquitoes to-night!" "Well! you know you can't sleep there near my bed. Just take that Chair off as far as you can." Which he did, not in the least abashed.

The Farmers wife was busy chatting, and chopping up the leaves of the grass cloth plant for the pigs.—It was 10 o'clock, and as they always get up by 4, I thought she might as well go to bed, and let me sleep. But she chopped, and chopped. So presently I thought I might as well watch her from under the Mosquito curtains, and had a heavenly night with a blanket over me, and such a breeze, till towards morning it actually blew the curtains from off me. Then a man passed with a torch, and all the dogs barked furiously. Presently the Farm people got up, lit their fire, and the men came outside to wash in the dawn. Walnuts began to fall here and there from the tree above me. The wind blew more and more, and I wondered what would be the result if a Walnut happened to fall on my eye. Till at last I thought it prudent to go inside, and finish up with two more hours of undisturbed sleep in the fresh morning air.

July 25th. A. came out quite late, and tells me two Swedish Missionaries have just been killed by the people about 100 miles from Hankow. It seems placards were put up telling them, they would be killed on a certain feast day, if they did not go away. But they could not believe it. The Magistrate asked them to take refuge in his Yamen, but said he could not restrain the people.

They stayed on in their house, the mob chased them out, and finally killed them. We do not know how. Hankow is in great excitement.

July 26th. A cool night and very cool morning. The Cook declared himself very ill, one of the Coolies also ill. Our first European guest, since we came here June 29th—an Agent of the Scotch Bible Society Felt as if I hardly knew what to say to him, when he rode out. The young man from the Yuen family again joined us on the hill, bringing a cousin, and another Poney, so there were 4 Ponies altogether there. The two young men came back uninvited to refreshment, and like two boys ate up every one of our cakes, trying to help themselves, when I was not looking.

July 27th. Cook again not well. A cool day! Thunderstorm all round in distance. Went again towards the Chai (Fortress of Refuge) and watched the thunderstorms, indicating distinctly the relative distance of the different Ranges. I estimate we see 7 to the south, one even beyond the—said to be 7000 ft. high—Golden Buddha mountain, and three to the West. The sunshine, silvery through clouds, and a large Lotus pond below looked like a silver pond, the dark large Lotus leaves standing out finely against it, and looking in the thickest part, as if they were mixed with silver flowers.

Our poor black Pointer pup has become nothing but skin and bone. We do not know what is the matter with him, but are trying a Chinese cure of Liquorice. The long haired Terrier was washed to-day, and the Soldier Coolie and I spent some hours over taking animals out of him. Between each pair of toes he had at least two Ticks, between some, three or four. I spend hours over him every day, but have not looked at his paws, thinking he would be sure to walk lame, if there were anything the matter with them.

July 28th. A. got off early, and when I got up at 7 found it still so cool, the Thermometer marking only 79, I thought I would take a few minutes stroll before breakfast, but the air is so moist that I came back soaked with perspiration and had to change every thing and rub myself dry. A very heavy day! Dark clouds over Chungking, and the darkness gradually creeping up to us like a heat mist. Found the little pond, into which the spring from which we get our water falls, full of frogs, small, very finely shaped and bright green. Birds flew in and out of the sitting-room to-day, as if troubled by the weather. Started at 1, P.M. for Chungking, a luxuriance of vegetation, Sun flowers dangling their leaves wearily amongst Rice in ear, Indian Corn, Millet, French Beans, Taro, and Lotus. Last two, banked up in mud in their ponds, alone looking as if not in want of more water; some Lotus already being pulled up for the roots. Found the River much risen, and flowing so fast I was not surprised there was considerable difficulty about getting a boat. We had to wait some time, send some way to look for boats and then only one big boat to be had. It at first refused to take us, but at last consented for 180 Cash, three times the large sum we usually pay. Coolies pay 8 cash a head. After we had been 10 min. in the boat, we were a good deal further down River than when we started, the towing rope having been let go by the Trackers, lest they should be dragged into the stream off a steep bank. The Cook then wanted to persuade me to go back. But for his pressure before I do not think I should ever have started. I did not like to go back now, and a great deal thanks to his exertions we got to the other side at last in five minutes under two hours. We then found that another boat had slipped its towline, as we had, in the morning, and three men out of the eight in her had been drowned, and A. had sent a Coolie to warn me not to try to cross the River, as it was so dangerous. But owing I suppose to the state of the Water he had not got over in time. It felt quite cold crossing the River, and the people say this sudden rise in it is owing to the melting of the snow in Thibet. Last time it was rain in Yunnan.

July 29th. Sitting on the Shai Tai, or Drying Place on the top of our house with A., watching the Thunderstorms all round—yet none arriving—he noticed a Coolie, one of the Callenders from the Adjacent Dyer's on his Shai Tai ***Ko Towing*** to the Thunder! Actually bought some grapes at the door, not quite ripe yet, but very nearly so, and in fine bunches. Had a dish of Lotus roots shredded, and sweetened with sugar for dinner. It was rather nice, seemed intended to be eaten with Chicken stewed with Cucumbers, Ginger, and a kind of Cabbage—the soup of this Chicken is perfectly dilicious. The mixture seemed curious, but pleasing.

July 31st. Meant to cross yesterday, but the River very high. Then it came on to rain, and in the end the Boy was too ill to go. Next day I settled to start with only Cook and Water Coolie, but the latter was so ill he sent a substitute. The Chinese seem to suffer quite as much as, if no more than we do from this oppressive weather. We crossed very high up, the water being smoother there, banked up by that below. But the bridge, crossing an affluent, that used to stand so high up, was still under water, only the tops of the stone stanchions rising from the Parapet visible above the water. Felt delightfully fresh at the Farm, and in the afternoon went for quite a long ride, and saw a pond of Lotus out in flower, but quite small blossoms, about half the size of those in Japan.

August 5th. The last few days we have had visitors, and my time has been too much taken up for more than admiring exquisite cloud effects in the extensive landscape on all sides of us, as the Thunderstorm threatened, but did not arrive. Yesterday however at last one did, and I think must have thoroughly washed out even Chungking. We were only on the fringe of it, but our Spring is replenished, and in a few minutes the Thermometer fell from 85 to 77. A. arrived with a violent attack of lumbago, which seems common here so we only went for a very little stroll, and wishing to sit at a view point with a fresh breeze asked a cottage near by to lend us a form to sit upon. The little boy, who brought it, and who replied with all the correct polite phrases when politely addressed, asked as a great favour if we would buy six eggs of them. They had only six. Our Coolie replied at once we could not think of buying less than ten at a time, but we insisted on buying six eggs of the little man, and he presently appeared with them, and was apparently too much delighted with two small foreign cakes even to recollect his manners. The storm has brought down a great many walnuts, and the little boy of the Farm, who kept me awake last night by his groaning—he has a horrible skin disease over both legs, especially under the kness —brought me four with great delight. A thunderstorm with occasional down pours began at 10 and went on

View from Fir Woods.

till 4. Till then the air felt heavy. We went for a ramble among the Fir woods to the South. Two of our servants asked leave to go—as the one said in Chinese "to reverence the Divinity," as the other in English "to a four man tiffin" at a Festival in a Temple near by, to which we yesterday evening saw a man staggering along under a heavy load of rice. Several country people returning from it came and sat about on the Threshing floor, and bright faced, very respectable looking women tried to talk to me. Then with that want of delicacy so conspicuous in Chinese, when I went to change my dress in our bedroom, came to the window to stare in, which they would not like done to themselves. So I shut the blinds with indignation. Scorpio, Cassiopeia and the Great Bear conspicuous in the evening, but the gentle Szechuan mist seems to temper the brilliancy of the stars here generally, as it mercifully does that of the sun.

August 6th. A crisp Autumnal feeling in the air, and the Thermometer actually 74 when we got up, which it has not been since July 3rd, when for two days we had it cool here. It was last 74 in Chunking on June 21st, a regular rainy day. To-day with fresh northerly breeze, bright sunshine, and exquisite blue sky with white fleecy Summer clouds we thought we could not be better off than at our Farm. I went to the back of the hill before breakfast, such a fresh, delicious breeze, and the golden Buddha Mountain—said to be from 4 to 6 days journey away, reports differ—absolutely clear all along its flat back, with only one or two white clouds rising from behind it, and threatening to overshadow it, as the day progresses. The Farm people unhusking their Indian Corn, so now no more roasted or baked Cobs, but Baba instead, as they call the hot cakes made of the flour, which we so enjoyed on the way to Thibet last year. Pink Crape Myrtle seems over, and now we have only White Hibiscus, and Ferns, and one red Rose on the table. The village Schoolmaster paid us several visits, and with him a young man in a shabby long black gown, whom I took for his assistant but who said his family owned the Chai, the Refuge Fortress, that crowns and connects the two tops of the highest hill in these party. He says they paid 20,000 Taels to build it 150 years ago and would sell it now for 80,000. There are Rice fields attached bringing in 600 Taels a year, His home is behind and below the Chai, and he says 100 people live in it. Other people tell us it is a very handsome house with a fine garden, so we were glad he asked us to go there. The Schoolmaster seemed a very merry sort of character. To-day was the great day for all the seeds, Baskets full of Indian Corn being unhusked, and Red and Black Peas being first spread in the sun, and pitchforked about as if to make hay, and then gathered into baskets. The beauty of the day tempted me to take several Photos, but I think I suffered afterwards from exposing myself to the sun. In the evening went up the hill, and found the view again beautifully clear. Coming down one of the Coolies began to dance about and jump, as if he saw a snake. I had no doubt but he did. But when he exclaimed "Why it must have weighed so many catties!" and moved his hands so as to indicate something, that neither tallied with the probable length nor breadth of a sanke I began to doubt. A. said he must have seen a hare, dwelling particularly on the length of its ears. A number of big birds were going to roost in a grove of firs. They looked like Pheasants, but the Coolies said one could not eat them, so I think they must have been Jays. They seemed very restless, and were flying about a good deal.

August 7th. Went into Cungking do-day so as to read the incoming Mail before the outgoing Mail went out. 92 there felt very hot after 72 at the Farm in the Morning, and the Mail was as usual here a disappointment. Not as many letters as we expected, and not one single newspaper. It will be 4 weeks to-morrow

Monastery with Pagoda.

since one has reached us. The head of the Counting house invited me to a dinner his wife and the Comprador's wife were giving at the Roman Catholic Guild garden. But I had to come back to the Farm. The Coolies turned cross and lazy, and two substitutes had to be got at the last moment. Turned aside on the way back to see some fields of Ginger, we saw when first planted near by the great Monastery with the Pagoda. It seems to be a sort of cane, and is only about a foot high yet. I am told it should grow to 2 ft. It is very carefully planted in perfectly straight rows, with 5 in. trenches between the rows kept apparently full of mud, but much lower than the plant. An odour of ginger seems to hang over it all, but I could not detect any ginger taste in the leaf. Got home in the dark, seeing one or two glowworms on the way.

August 8th. Called on the Yuen family. Everyone was in Chungking, but the great grandmother of our young friend of the Poney. She told us she was 77, but seemed to see and hear quite well, and spoke refreshingly distinctly, but said she could not accompany us round the garden, as she could not walk, and that there were no flowers there now. The Camelia trees with such magnificent flowers, when we were here before, now many of them had white and variegated leaves. What I had taken for red leaves from outside turned out to be Crape Myrtle looking like a red flame, and there was one Gardenia and one flower of a coral colour, whose name, I do not know though I have often seen it before. The servant picked some orchids for me, which though not very pretty I was delighted to see, as I had long been watching the leaves, wondering what they would develope into. Our Coolies were chiefly interested in a big coffin, which was being got ready for the old lady. A wanted me to tell her I had seen it, and compliment her upon it, as is the etiquette in China; but I really could not. She had quite the manners, and I thought the hands of a lady, but was dressed like any poor woman. The servants examined and admired every bit of my Chinese dress, more than I have ever been examined in European dress. They evidently like it much better and think much more of it. There was a water colour picture of one of the Ancestors in grand official dress hanging as a Kakemono on the wall. It looked as if it were an excellent

Country House near Chungking.

likeness, and the face stood out, so that one could hardly believe it was not in relief.

Our Threshing floor was again spread with Peas to-day, and beautiful cobs of Indian Corn, which were raked about preparatory to unhusking them like so much hay. Certainly this Farm seems to produce everything. The Farmer has been away the last day or two. It seems he is carrying on his Coal business at the biggest mine near here, buying the coal on the spot, and retailing it in Chunking. If he had not such an energetic wife he would have enough on his hands. As it is, she seems to manage the Farm, and the children. She will not consent to the little boy with the bad legs going into the Mission Hospital, declaring he is a very difficult child to manage, and would be sure to cry and be naughty there. Besides who would give him his food? Probably it is incredible to her that the Hospital would, and if she did believe it, she would at once [suspect some deep design underlying such open handedness, as of course there is; i.e. alienating the patients from the Faith of their Fathers, and predisposing them to another in its place, which probably this satisfied-with-things-as-they-are woman like most Chinese women would regard as the most dreadful thing. The poor little fellow cannot be cured without going into a Hospital however, as he must be kept perfectly quiet, so probably he will go on moaning at nights, according as the weather affects his legs. Just now he is better.

August 13th. Since I last wrote in my Diary a very unfortunate incident has occurred. Our little dog's barking had annoyed us so much, that in order to get some sleep at night I shut him up in one basket inside another on the 9th. That night it was rainy and so chilly, we shut the front door for almost the first time since we have been here. But the next night, as it was very close as well as rainy I left the front door open, and yet shut up poor little Jack as before. Next morning as A. woke he said: "It is really no use sleeping out here. I feel so heavy, just as if I were going to bed, instead of getting up." But my attention was distracted from him by seeing my clothes, which I had left lying tidily on the top of one of our travelling baskets, all in confusion on the earth floor and some of the contents of the basket lying in the dirt too. Then I saw some of the clothes out of the Cupboard on the floor, and on the window sill the brush and comb, which I had left in one corner well inside the window, quite in another place outside the wooden bars, and the Candle stick also outside the bars, and as it struck me the candle much shorter than I had left it. Then on the other side of the bed there were my dark glasses and belt also lying on the floor, and underneath the bed, exactly underneath where I had been sleeping, the tray, which had been taken out of one of the baskets and evidently put there during the night. Quite bewildered, not sure if I were dreaming or not, I looked into the sitting room to see the Lamp, where I had left it, but the shade and chimney both by the side of it, instead of on it, as if some one had lighted that too. A very little further investigation shewed both our Watches gone, A's Compass, both our Eye-glasses, all the Spoons and Forks, and Sheets and Table cloths we had brought out with us, also all A's Chinese clothes, and a good many of my European clothes. But one of the Coolies looking about presently brought back all the latter together with some Towels and Napkins, thrown down into some Indian Corn hard by and soaked with rain. The behaviour of our little dog was very peculiar. He did not bound out of his basket as usual, but sat quite stupidly, letting all the people of the Farm crowd into the room, and talk and look about, whereas generally he has to be held even if the Farmer's wife comes in, so indignant is he at any one but our own servants coming amongst our things. He seemed very sleepy, and presently sat himself down, and watched the door of the next room, but interfered with no one. My own impression was at once he had been drugged. But, if a dog's gestures are to be believed, this poor little fellow said "I am very weary, but look behind that door, and you will find your things." The room he was looking at however was that occupied by the Farmer, his wife, and family, and it seemed impossible to suspect them. The Farmer as one of the Guardians of Order in the District went off at once to report the occurrence. And presently arrived a local Yamen Runner (tipstaff) to hear the story, and take note of every thing, which however he did not seem to do, but just sat about a little, and then went away. Some hours afterwards arrived three men in Chairs from the Magistrate's Yamen with a great following, One of the oddest things to me was, how quiet every one was! No exclamations nor lamentations! No attenpt on the part of the Farm people to clear themselves from suspicion! These men did take note of every thing, and especially wanted a careful list and description of the things stolen, that they might search the pawn shops. Soon after that we went into town, and as it rained I did not come out again till yesterday, whən another accident occurred. Our little Poney had grown so fresh by itself here, it set off to gallop up the hill at the back with me, actually kicking up its heels with pleasure at being out again, in spite of the steepness. I rode it quite to the top of a mountain we had not been up before, where we found the Farm children gathering what looked like the smallest and most gnarled of Crab Apples, but which they get off a bush, that grows along the ground. They were munching them with great satisfaction, and as usual eager to offer me some, but I could' detect no flavour at all. I got off however to enjoy the view and specially red sunset, then gave the Poney to our old man to lead down the hill, intending to mount him again presently, and go for a little further ride along the road. But the little Poney said to itself "That is not the nearest way home. You mistake," twtiched his head loose from the old man, kicked up his heels, and went careering along the hill side. Very pretty the little thing—11 hands 4 and perfectly proportioned—looked doing so, and fortunately there were no worse consequences than a broken bridle. As we have another to replace that, till it is mended, that does not so much matter. But I have never now any notion what o'clock it is without a watch, and our supply of Table cloths also seems sadly short. And though last year travelling to Thibet I did my hair for three months without a looking glass, yet I am vexed to miss the convenient Hand glass out of my travelling bag. And now I find the thieves did not throw my belt on the floor, till they had wrenched the buckle off. A. says Chinese thieves are supposed to burn something to make one sleep. Without something of the kind it is incredible how we could have slept through so much rummaging of two baskets, and a cupboard, also a drawer, and a box opened. The latter had one of my slippers stuck in it it to make it shut noiselessly. Some of the things belonging to the Farm people were taken also, in especial two Candlesticks, and two Straw hats; but they make strangely little fuss about them. I have forgotten to mention that their dog, which generally sleeps outside and barks, was shut up that night because of the rain. But they say it did bark, and one of them got up to see what was the matter and saw nothing. Our other dog was sleeping in the kitchen at the back on this particular night, also on account of the rain. This morning I went for quite a ride before breakfast, determined to take it out of the Poney, and myself. But there was very little breeze even on the tops of the hills, and the air felt heavy, as if another Thunderstorm were under way. They are pulling up the Indian Corn near the house, and already rows of well grown Pepper Plant stand revealed, and in other places Taro.

August 16th. Sunflowers everywhere, but by no means generally looking East. To-day the air sweet with Kwei Hoa flower (Olea Fragrans), and a branch in our room, also a lovely breeze. Yesterday all the air round the house heavy with the smell of the three Cess-pools, on which all the fertility of this light rocky soil depends, but which one often wishes further. Walnuts falling in showers yesterday I slept outside again last night, but there was not a breath of air; the dogs barked dreadfully, the Cicadas shrilled and shrieked like Policemen's rattles, and the sheet lightning seemed continuous. I think I ought to have arranged from the first to mark in my Diary any day, on which there was neither lightning nor thunder—but I doubt if there has been one—as also when the children at the Farm were not one or other beaten. To-day the little boy screamed so, I went out to see what he was being beaten with, as I one day saw his mother chasing and threatening him with a large log,

Entrance to Monastery.

such as one puts on the fire. But to-day it seemed only a decent sized stick. The whacks however sounded serious, and I was glad to see his father interceding for him.—Very red sunsets both the last nights! The Poney again nearly ran away from the man leading him yesterday. Having tasted the delights of scampering loose once he wants to repeat them apparently, so I took him out for a ride again this morning. The most amusing thing is to see him roll, when he comes in, directly the saddle is taken off. These small Western poneys seem to enjoy it, as chidren do. Our poney looks very much like a bady—but for its very serious, intelligent face—lying down in its fern bed at night.—It looks such an absurdly small thing to ride then. But it can do its 30 miles a day with ease, carrying weight too. The children and Farm people have been munching Millet stalks lately. They seem to me like a very inferior kind of Sugar cane, with the one advantage of being much softer. They have picked all their grapes quite hard, as the leaves of the Varnish tree, on which it has twined itself, are too thick for them to ripen they say. But I doubt if they know the difference between ripe and unripe fruit. For they always gather it unripe. And they seem quite to enjoy these grapes, with the enjoyment only heightened by seeing my wry face, when they persuade me to taste one.

August 17th. Last night everyone was requisitioned to strip the Indian Corn off the cobs, as they do not hang them up here to dry in the fashion we found so picturesque between Fulin and Yacheo last year, when the Villages were all dressed with them, golden and red. I have at last found out why they grow the Hibiscus, whose delicate white blossoms are just now in perfection. It is to make a cooling ***tisane,*** for which purpose they strip off the green calyx, and split the flower open to get out the stamens etc. A Sunflower near the house is actually over 12 ft. high. The Thermometer was 82 early this morning, hotter than it has been for a long while, but it does not feel so hot from having a fresh breeze. We slept outside again, undismayed by thoughts of Walnuts falling on our heads. They do not seem to have any idea of shaking the tree, but just pick up what falls. In this way however I annexed about 20 yesterday to send in to friends in town, who have a difficulty about getting fresh walnuts.

"Garnered Maize."

I have only been hit yet once, though we are always sitting and sleeping under the tree, and that was on the arm where it did not matter. One of the married daughters has been making sandals for A. and me, soles and all, quite a success! She came to discuss a night dress bag, which I want worked in cross stich as elaborately as her little boy's Pinafore. She says it will take her a month, and asks 1000 Cash (3s.). But I know that is, because I paid 1000 Cash for one our Tailor got worked for me. So I offer her 600 Cash, a friend of mine having had one worked for 400 Cash, but I think probably less covered with work than I want mine.

Begging Priest counting Cash.

August 19th. The cook actually gave us Hibiscus Soup yesterday, by way of a cooler. The flavour was rather agreeable. Yesterday was a very hot day, and the Head of the Counting House sent out word to A. he had better not go in before Monday it was so hot. Probably no one would do any business in such weather. Even here at the farm our own servants were all stripped to the waist, except the Boy of course, and have now given up bundling on something to appear before me. The evening before, when we came in from our walk we found the two young men from the Yuen family sitting round a table with the people of the Farm drinking Chinese Spirits neat. They had brought me some flowers, and wanted A. to shew them his Typewriter, and were very pressing that we should go to their house to-day, as they were over in Chungking, when we went before. So we went some time after five. First pause outside the gate, whilst A. put on a long gown, he having ridden. Then further pause, whilst the servants put on their clothes. On going inside we found a number of Paper Horses, Chairs, and Attendants, and a Taoist Priest, chanting all by himself, in the entrance Hall, all being hung round with pictures of Ancestors. It was the anniversary of the Grandfather's, or great Grandfather's birthday. He died 8 years ago aged 83. One of the young men received us, not our Number 5 young gentleman, who was out riding. Then came in a whole lot of women. They did not bow to me, nor ask me to sit down, and were dressed quite commonly, just in long jackets and trousers of the commonest materials. So it did not occur to me they were the ladies of the house. But the young man who was talking to A. on the other side of the great Entrance Hall now came to the women's side and introduced them. One was his mother; she, I gathered was the principal lady, who entertained us the first time we were there. One was number 5's mother. Then there was his Sister, and his

Ladies of the House.

Wife, and possibly some more, whom I confused with the Servants. Number 5's mother was put forward to entertain me, a tall, thin woman, not at all like her stout son of genial, honest broad face. But she had a bright countenance. Walking about a little I asked the ladies leave to look into an adjoining bedroom, and we all went in, and they served me with Tea and Sponge cakes there. They examined my clothes, lifting up my petticoat etc. just as unceremoniously as poor wonen do. Whilst I was talking to her mother I felt Number 5's Sister fingering the plaits on my dress at the back, quite without any apology. As far as I could make out Number 5's mother told me she got up at ten, and went to bed at ten, and did nothing all day, except smoke, and ***shwa*** that is "amuse herself." She could not work, she said, nor cook, and did not read. I did not ascertain whether she could not. The two young girls read, she said. When we came out again Number 5 had come in. He had been thrown from his Poney. He and the other young man led the way to the flower garden. The ladies followed through two Courtyards on there tiny feet with difficulty, then declined coming further. We passed the Coffin of the old lady, who had also come in later to receive us, but from another side, and stood apart by herself all the time. They laughingly said it was hers, and one of them stretched herself back to shew how the old lady would lie stretched out in it. There were some 10 or more paper boxes full of paper cash to be sent after the old Grandfather by being burned, that being the Taoist Post. And as we came back we saw specially good Calligraphists writing letters to the deceased. The very hot day had become quite cool with a beautiful fresh wind, looking as if it must turn to rain each minute. But the young men were eager for us to see a very fine Crape Myrtle tree of which they declared the leaves trembled, if one only scratched the trunk. As all the leaves were trembling in the wind we could not decide, if this was more than a Legend. Then Number 5. actually tried to swarm up the tree to get me some of the lovely pink blossom. He seemed quite irrepressible and next insisted on lifting up my Chair with me and Jack in it and he and one of our Coolies carried me about 100 yards. After which the two young men came a little further to see how our poney frisked along even with A. on his back. We came home, and sat out in the moonlight, revelling in the cool breeze, till we actually found it too chilly. We had to sleep inside, and the wind quite wailed before I got to sleep. This morning heavy rain, coming in at 3 places in the Sitting room.

August 22nd. Sunday the 20th being again a rainy day we went into town in the evening. The country people were busy picking Peppers as we passed along, and there were many little fires of paper Cash by the River side for the Spirits of those drowned. No boat would take us at first, but at last one said it would for 300 Cash; we generally pay 60, Coolies paying rather more than 8 cash, now the water is so high. Rather to our surprise we heard the Cook without any attempt at bargaining at once promise 300 Cash. But arrived on the other side he only gave 120. At last after a good deal of fuss, as usual, he gave 160 Cash. That's the only way to manage, he said, when asked for on explanation. "If I had given the 160 at once, the man would not have taken it. And if I had not promised the 300 in the first instance they would have run away, and you would have got no boat to cross over in. Now, as you saw they were perfectly satisfied with the 160 in the end." And so really it appeared. Went shopping yesterday, and was nearly choked in the streets by the acrid odour of the quantity of Red Peppers being fried. In the afternoon going to the

Outside the City Gate.

"Friends Mission" Country House found nearly all the Missionaries of the place out there, after having been nearly suffocated by the smoke of the innumerable little fires of imitation Paper money over the graves outside the City Gate. Coming back when it was darker, there was still the same smarting smoke, but the fires looked very pretty. There were many of them all about the vast Grave-yard that stretches on all sides but the River side up to the City Gates; but there seemed, as far as I could see, to be an extra number in the Paper Burning enclosures just outside the gate I went out by. It felt beautifully fresh and cool getting back into the country this morning. There seems to be no nutriment in the City air just now, one feels quite faint breathing it.

August 26th. Yesterday the Farmer's wife brought in all the large packets of paper cash, that the eldest son has been so busy directing in his best handwriting for some days past to the Grandfather, Uncle, all the dead relations to the number of 11. He had a list to do it by with the amount of Cash etc. to be sent to each carefully calculated. The Farmer came in and stood the packets in rows along three sides of the table; then with the help of the little boys a number of Chop sticks were brought in, and a dinner laid, with cups of wine all round. The Farmer prostrated himself before it all, and the ancestral tablets three times, having previously carefully lighted a little row of Joss sticks and burnt some Incense. He then very reverentially burnt some paper on the floor before the table, and poured on the floor two cups of wine; after which the whole dinner was carried away to be eaten, and the envelopes to be burnt, which they were in the evening, when they made a cheerful blaze. They had wanted us to dine with them that day, but A. did not come out till evening and I had visitors. The Yuen family had sent us an invitation to dinner the day before, but the servants sent back word A. was in Chungking. I as it happened was walking a Missionary, who had come out for fresh air and exercise, all over our hills from 9 to 1. It seemed wonderful one could do this on August 25th, especially as it was sunny. But the breeze was delightful. There are so many dragon flies about now, and of much more brilliant colouring than earlier. The grasshoppers also are very big and numerous now. We especially admired a big green one, with a reddish head, and a broad amber stripe all down its back. The Farm family seem at last to have finished unhusking their Indian Corn, the business of so many evenings past.

September 3rd. Last Tuesday, August 29th seems to have been the hottest day this year, and then in one sick room in Chungking the Thermometer fell from over 100 to 70 within the 12 hours. Here it did not rise above 87 although it felt much hotter, and already by luncheon time it was getting cooler. Then rose such a wind one

Chungking from "Little" River.

could hardly walk against it, and next morning it felt so cold I hurried to Chungking to find the Thermometer only 72, heap on clothes and generally feel very chilly. The day before that I saw some Tea bushes in flower, and to-day coming out Rice Harvest seemed going on merrily, the rice being beaten with a stick, directly it is gathered, behind a screen in each field. Yesterday the Farmer's wife came to see us in her new clothes, begging us to interfere to protect her, as the Magistrate is insisting on her declaring the present whereabouts of the man, whom she had here weaving, before the Robbery, and of whom she now says she knows nothing. Of course we will not, as we thought from the first he was very likely an accomplice. Every other foreigner, or Chinese dependent upon a Foreigner, who has been robbed, seems to have either recovered the stolen articles, or been compensated for them by the local authorities, so I think we ought to get something. Yesterday I spent bargaining for Counterpanes with quaint patterns in blue and white, to be used as Table cloths, and Pillow cases for Chair backs. A Composition with the pattern drawn or stamped on it is used as a Stencil plate. Then with a large brush lime is passed over the pattern. After which the cloth is dried and then when quite dry the white lime is brushed off. Thus the oftener they are washed the better

Cargo Junk.

they are said to look. I got a large Table cloth for one dollar, a third less than the man asked, but very likely too much. Some Pongee silks were brought for us to see, some undyed, some dyed the most beautifully artistic shades, so that I longed to buy them all. They are about 3 Taels 6 Mace or 10s. the piece of 60 Chinese feet (24 yds.) of about 17½ in. wide. Such are the City amusements! but out here the fresh breeze feels so invigorating as more than to compensate. However, a Junk 3 months out from Ichang (the nearest point to which steamers run) is said at last to be arriving with our things, so I must go into the City to see them, as also to make sure that the Tailor puts the silk wadding I am paying for (instead of cotton or half cotton) into the Silk wadded Dressing gown I am having made as a wedding present.

September 5th. All yesterday watched two Tailors putting silk wadding into dressing gown, and smoothing down the edges with dabs of cotton wadding. Then having announced that it would take eight days to finish it, the dressing gown was carried off and I cannot see anything to prevent them from substituting cotton for silk in the privacy of their own apartment, if the spirit so moves them. The Head Tailor however is a Christian, and his father before him, so he ought to be above such dishonesty. He has, however, like the equally Christian Godown-man a perfectly inscrutable face, which always makes me think the latter descended from Mahommedans; but though coming from Yunnan, where there are so many, he says he is not. We came out to the Farm in the morning. The country looks rather yellow now with just stubble where the Rice fields and the exquisitely graceful tall Millet were. The Indian Corn is also all cut down, and the Sunflowers, standing up tall and somewhat wide apart in sort of groves, give the effect of a garden run quite wild. Some turnips and also some Beans are already planted out but they are barely sprouting as yet.

Septenber 7th. Yesterday went for quite a ride along the hill tops, and then on by the Fuchow Road, round by the Dwarf

Country Road.

oak walk, and back along the hill tops. It was extraordinary to see what places the Poney carried me down; they tried my nerve once or twice, especially as the poney generally stopped at the top to see if I would get off. But it then carried me down apparently with no difficulty. Once or twice when I made a mistake about the path the little creature tried with all its might to go the right way, although as far as I know it has only been twice before in those parts, at all. There were biggish drops of rain most of the time with violent gusts of wind, so that I had to take off my hat, and by the time I got home it was regularly raining. The storm only began, however, as night came on, such a violent wind the Walnuts fell in showers, the children like merry grigs running in and out to pick them up. Then one of our blinds was violently blown to and broken, next a branch crashed off the Walnut tree. I had to bolt all the doors to keep the draught out, the first time since we have been here, that we have done more than put the doors to. The rain seemed pretty heavy, but I was relieved that it only came in, in one place, to the sitting room, where I decided to sleep, as less damp then the bedroom. We have almost given up using the latter room except as a dressing room in spite of all the precautions A. has taken to make it dry and airy. Mud floors on a precipitous hill side, when it rains, are not suited to European constitutions. But I did not feel it as cold as the Farm people, who looked blue, and ran about in their excitement declaring they were so cold; the children with their clothes tucked up to their thighs, lest they should wet them. Jack was not satisfied until a basket was brought him with straw, on which he straightway curled himself up inside, as comfortable as any cat, whilst the little Poney was led to his bed to do likewise.

September 11th. We returned to the Farm again on the 9th to find the most perfect weather, bright sunshine, crisp, pure air, a pleasant breeze, and a clear blue sky. Spent almost all Saturday out on the hills. In the evening went to call on one of the Missionaries, who, having found our air very reviving, have now taken rooms in the same house the China Inland occupied last year, some 150 feet lower than we are, and nearer the village, but a grander house than that we occupy and with a garden enclosed by a wall, which they happily think a great advantage. I should not like it at all, as it shuts out the breeze, and seems to shut in the Mosquitoes. Our friends were out, but the people of the house received us, as if our call were to them, the lady of the house having amber bracelets and very fine manners. Our Landlord, who had formerly been her tenant, was there deeply engaged with some Christian tracts. He had seemed really interested and for a long time pursued the conversation which a Church Missionary, staying with us, began owing to the Farmers curious mistake, thinking the three Old Women washing, each with a wash tub in front of her, in Sunlight Soap's Advertisement were three English Buddhas sitting on Lotus Flowers and with high caps for Glories. But besides being anxious about Religion he and our Hostess were voluble on the subject of the misery the Officials were bringing on the District by searching for our stolen property. They quarter their Runners on the various houses in the neighbourhood, and one poor man we were now told had to sell his clothes in order to provide dinner for these men. They begged us to interfere. But this is the Chinese way of forcing the people, some of whom they know must be in the secret, to give information. There was a really beautiful bush of Marvel-of-Peru in full variegated flower, and some red Lilies and Marshal Niels and Balsams, so the garden looked gay. A. had before been by our Landlord's invitation with him to dine and **Shwa** at the T'u Shan Temple. As Chinese have generally an ulterior object he thought perhaps he was taken as a witness, for the object of the visit to the Temple was to get the Priests there to pay for some grain they had had from our Farm. The Farmer came away however unsuccessful, and took occasion to tell A. what an idle lot the Priests were, and how he himself would never contribute to Temples, but to good roads, bridges, free Ferries and the like. A lady Missionary had been spending the day with us, and he wanted to know what her object was in coming, and how much she got paid for it. A. told him, which was the truth in her case, that she was very rich and got paid nothing, but only came for love of the people, anxious to do them good, adding that he himself told her, she had much better not come here, but go home and do good there, as the people here did not want her, and did not like her. This only to make her position intelligible to the Farmer—a most difficult thing to do, for it is an incredible position to a Chinaman. But the Farmer exclaimed "Who does not like her? Only bad people. All decent people must be grateful to her for coming to help the poor people." And when she went away the Farmer's wife presented her with two Pomegranates off the one tree, and some fresh Walnuts. Yesterday evening the Farmer came in with his Tract, greatly troubled; his eyes were not good, and the print was too small, for him to read much of it. He hoped I liked a bunch of red Lilies he had brought me, and now what was **Shang Ti** (Supreme Ruler)? Wasn't He the same as Heaven-and-Earth? and as the Lord of Heaven? The latter is the name the Roman Catholics give God in Chinese, the former the Chinese name for Him, and Heaven-and-Earth is either another name for God, or a God the Chinese thus worship. I only know just enough Chinese to say Supreme Ruler and Lord of Heaven were one and the same, and created Heaven and Earth. "That's it, said the Farmer, that's it!" But I wish I could convey the extreme reverence with which he spoke, and the way in which he waved his hand around, as if to signify Heaven and Earth and all things. "Images are no good," he continued and then went on with a long diatribe against them which I could not follow. "They are no good, are they?" he asked eagerly. "They are made of wood," I said hesitatingly, for I know so few words. "Yes, of wood, or of clay," said he. But he was evidently anxious to have his book read to him, and I could only read isolated characters here and there, so he went off to study it by himself. He has just the same type of face as the High Priest at the Temple we stayed at last year on the top of the sacred Mountain of Omi, and is evidently naturally of a religious turn, and quite unsatisfied by Buddhism. But as A. had had to go into town to send off his letters, having suddenly recollected that, owing to its being a short moon, Mail night was one night earlier than usual there was no one to talk to him.

The sunset was beautiful last night, red fading into various tints of orange and yellow, a sort of Aurora Borealis as so many nights before sending out bunches of rays in different directions, some straight at me, as I sat on a new hill top to witness it. But to-day the disagreeables of Farm Life began again. I had been sitting outside, thinking how beautifully fresh and pure the air was, and how delightful that now with a milder sun one could really enjoy out of door life, and not be boxed up in the house all through the daylight hours. Thc farm people had as usual been breakfasting outside sitting on low benches round a very little, low table, the children sitting on the high threshold, all busy with their bowls. But when this was over, men came with loads, and there seemed to be a great re-mixing of the liquid manure almost as valuable for farm produce as the solid, for which last they pay a quarter of a dollar every two buckets if they have to buy it. The smell, though only in whiffs at each fresh mixing, was really too objectionable, so I went inside.—In town the Pigs are now said to have got Swine fever, and to be dying by hundreds, so we have been cautioned not to eat Pork, and handed this caution on to our servants, who however are quite unimpressed. The cows are said for the second time to have gone to Gaol by the Magistrates orders, as they are accused of damaging the graves, which occupy all available pasture land outside the city. There is however a slight doubt as to whether this is not a fable of the Dairy-man's in order to raise the price of Milk, or account for some shortcoming. For each time that the cows are all said to be sent to prison some people get their milk all the same.

We are beginning to wonder whether the worrying the people round so much on the plea of our stolen goods is not in order to make them object to our going on building on the land we have rented near here.—Directly the robbery occurred one Missionary said he should not be surprised if it had been done by order of the Magistrate in order to say he could not undertake to protect foreigners outside the city walls.—This seems too elaborate a plot. But that they should utilise the theft to make us disliked in the neighbourhood would only be natural. We hear no more of having our money returned us for the piece of land we rented last year, and have not so far been allowed to build upon, nor of our being allowed to go on building, and the three months we were to spend at this farm in order to accustom the people to us et cetera, are nearly up. From the first, and all through indeed the country people have been only too friendly and cordial. It seems the Country people were so to those two Missionaries, who were murdered, and now they are all being tortured and ruined to make them also bring accusations against the two dead men. It makes one's blood boil to think of it; everyone who was in friendly relations with them is being persecuted, and the men from a distance, who killed them,—paid to do so of course—are untouched. I dare not let myself think of it in this heat and loneliness. I feel as if were I the friend of the murdered men, I must ask to be tortured in the place of those poor ignorant Chinese, who are being tortured out of all recognition.—But I cannot think of it.

Crimson Peppers and Indian Corn are spread out in the sun on the threshing floor, the latter unhusked, and now being carefully raked over and over, so as to be thoroughly dried.

September 13th. As we go up the mountain at the back so often and just the last bit is so slippery I took our strongest

Coolie, whom we sometimes call the Savage, because he is just a great, strong brute, to cut steps. There I heard the jingling of bells, and saw some members of the Yuen family were paying us a visit, and finding us out were sitting round a table with the Farm people. When I came down A. had arrived from the town, and after admiring their Ten Taels new saddle, a very handsome affair indeed, but so mounted up on their poney's back as to look very heavy our Cook brought out wine for the party. We did not know till afterwards that he had put half water with the Claret, and then added Sugar, both to make the wine go further, and to make it more acceptable to a Chinese palate. But for months afterwards the wine on this occasion was always referred to as the best foreign wine they had ever tasted. There were just four glasses for their party, and one for A. But our particular young friend was actually so polite as to offer his to me. I declined, but what interested me to observe was that one of the party promptly passed his glass on to the groom, who also had sat down on the same bench with him, our foreign chairs not going round for so large a party,—and the groom after having his drink handed it on again to one of the boys of the farm, so that everyone sitting round was included. The same with some cigars A. produced. Our young friend, having examined them with much interest, declined to smoke but one of his brothers, who had also already professed himself very ready to study English, if A. would give him lessons, smoke done for a while, then handed it on again, till it was passed from hand to hand like a Chinese pipe, each having a smoke in turn.

The married daughter of the Farm, who has been working, and most beautifully, a nightdress bag for me with a marriage procession on the back in cross stitch, has developed bad ophthalmia, and now can hardly see for it. We hear it is very much about. We feel greatly concerned. Great excitement among the boys, because our missionary friends are going to exhibit a Magic Lantern on Thursday evening outside the Temple. We have our table covered with red Guernsey Lilies now, with a few sweet smelling Orchids like monkey's faces intermixed.—We had guests to stay again yesterday. Unfortunately the dogs barked horribly at men passing by carrying coal, so it was difficult to sleep. And to-day again they are doing something to the various Cesspools, and the smell is horrible. The little boys are eating Sunflowor seeds, out of what look like gigantic Artichokes but are of course old Sunflowers.

September 17th. A. dreadful scene just now! Everyone has come and shouted at me with much gesticulation, apparently thinking that the way to make me understand was to make me deaf, but I cannot make out what it is about, except that it has something to do with our robbery. A man in a long, blue gown came first and sat down and waved his fan commandingly to all points of the compass, making such horrid faces I got the little Camera out to Photograph him. But on that he sat quite still, and was decidedly not worth taking. Then the mistress of the house wept, after evidently imploring my assistance; then dressed, and went across the River with the blue gowned man, and the daughter who is married unhappily, and was returning to her cruel husband, together with little, Hae Ching, who had made a special toilette for the occasion, got his hair all combed off his face, and tidily plaited with extra red cords twisted round it, together with what looked like an extra heavy basket of Farm Produce, Chickens, Sun Flowers etc. There was great regret that A. had already crossed the River, and apparently they are going to interview him in the first instance. I imagine the woman is to be cross examined at the Yamen about the Rebbery, but feel the more hard hearted, because not having been well lately and had a difficulty about sleeping, it is very trying to be so often disturbed by the dogs, and ihis morning very early having at last got into a thoroughly comfortable sleep I was awakened by poor little Jack barking with great determination, and someone, who had evidently just been coming in at our door retreating with a loud laugh—evidently some one belonging to the house. The night before everyone was up looking for thieves, one at least of whom they said was behind the house.—We sleep in the sitting room now, the earthy smell, and smell from the back being too bad in the bedroom, and as there is no window—nothing but the door—one requires to keep that open, unless the night is cold, which it was not last night.

Yesterday the day before this unintelligible but rather moving scene, was a beautiful day. A. came over early. And after breakfast we started with the little Poney between us, and actually got as far as the Gong, Gorge, going all the way along this range, without ever descending, most of the time in Oak and Fir Scrub with Bracken growing thickly and a delightful odour of we knew not what, but it smelt like Sweet Brier. The viws on either side as we went along the Table land at the top were very fine, and we saw the Chin Fo Shan and all the mountains to the South East well towards evening. The much heard of Hoa I Shan to the North, which I have only seen once all the time we have been out here, would not shew up. Tarchendo had his bridle taken off, and grazed beside us, when we stopped, but he was still a little lame because the cook galloped him along the paved road, whilst we were in town, brought him down, and fell off, himself getting covered with bruises. When I asked him, if he had not enjoyed his holiday from work, he presented a most pitiful appearance, and afterwards it all came out. Just now under my supervision he has been giving Tarchendo, so-called from the Thibetan name of Ta Chien Lu, where we bought him, a cold water bandage, using one of my long blue sandal cloths for the purpose, and the little pony looks quite smart and comfortable again with it on.

We stopped at a Cottage to have some water boiled to drink, as there was no good drinking water to be got all the way along and the sun had rather affected me, so that one bottle of lemonade between us and some Pears were not enough. The Coolies seemed very shy of asking anywhere for it, but Kung Tao the funny old Character, who attends upon the Poney, and is generally led about by it, rather than leads it, and who is known to all the country side, had some friends in a cottage near by, So we went there, and got a Pumelow as well as Hot Water. Then A. had a dip in one of the Head Pools for

Rice Fields and Opium Poppies.

irrigating the Rice Fields, very warm at the top and cool below, and our Soldier Coolie actually went in too, pronouncing it very cold.

Before we started yesterday we saw hanging up the leg of the Wild Boar, which we hunted one night, but did not kill. It has been killed of course whilst we have been away. So far that seems the only piece of it forthcoming, and that was smoked when we saw it.

The Missionary Magic Lantern Entertainment had only one fault we are told that it brought in so many people from the country round, who all stayed the night, and wanted breakfast next morning. Strangely enough there was a high wind that evening, so unusual in these parts, so it could not be outside as intended, but had to take place in the Temple. As the crowd inside were all bent npon seeing, and I did not want to stand in their way, and they also smelt strongly inside a building I soon went away, but the Farm people with whom I went to it seem to have enjoyed it, though they are so undemonstrative it is hard to tell, whether they were satisfied, or simply puzzled. Hae Ching gives a very good account of the Pictures and of what Jesus did and said, for in the second part the Slides were illustrative of His life. I quite nuderstand that, as people go on trying to convert Chinese and failing, they seize first one aid (?) and then another. But the Exhibition of Magic Lantern Slides ilustrative of the life of Jesus, of whom they have never heard, with what to them appear very comical clothes, and doing very funny things—in a Buddhist Temple too—to Chinese, does not commend itself to me. My belief is that Hospitals, Schools, Magic Lanterns, and all such quasi-bribes to hear about Christianity only lower Christianity in their eyes, as free Teas together with Gospel Addresses have lowered it in the eyes of the self respecting poor in the East of London.

We have got a new house and the Hong is moving in to it, so that we and our Household will remain alone in that we at present occupy in the City. This will give us more room, and some quiet. The noise has been very great of late. And I hope it may save our servants from all being corrupted by the free living ways of Szechuan business men, whose one idea seems to be dinner parties and wine drinking. When A. wanted to come across yesterday, the Boy never came to wait upon him. So enquiring he fouud he had not come in all night. When the Boy appeared he said with the greatest calm, he had been to dinner with the Carpenter night before, and taken too much wine. Not a muscle of his face expressed shame or confusion. But all Chinese think it rather grand than otherwise to drink much wine. The other day a very nicely dressed, most respectable women arrived out here to see us. She turned out to be the mother of the lame young man, who took his two very prettily dressed little girl twins to see the Dragon Festival from our boat, when I went, and brought them to pay their respects to me first. He is an outside dusiness man, receiving no Salary, but eating the Hong's Rice, and to be paid Commission on any business he gets. But it seems so far he has not got any. His mother was in great distress about him. She began by asking A. to give him a Salary, and pay it to her, as he brought nothing home for his little girls, his wife and herself. She had been in a good way of business, but his extravagance had ruined her, forcing her to sell first one thing, then another. Then she proceeded to beg A. to send him away, that is to employ him elsewhere, as she said he had bad Associates here, who led him astray, and that he was all the time *shwa*-ing with them, instead of with his excellent business connection. A. promised to do what he could, and in the first instance decided to exhort the young man, which he says he did with some sternness, but without making any roference to his mother's visit. Again, he said, though he watched the young man closely, having placed him in a strong light for the purpose, he found his countenance perfectly unperturbed and inscrutable.

The Tailor has now finished the wadded silk dressing gown, which I want to send B. as a present on his marriage. He has made all the alterations in it with equanimity, having started off by making it too tight everywhere, which they will think is what foreigners desire, and gradually having got it to something like Chinese looseness. But he now firmly declines to make any more foreign clothes. They give him too much anxiety he says. As there are plenty more Tailors, and he seems to be charging us more than other people pay I the less regret this.

September 19th. The dreadful scene is explained. When the poor Farmer's wife went in two days ago she knelt to A., for the discharged Weaver under torture has confessed to being the thief (people say falsely) but says he did it at the instigation of the nice, married eldest son ef the Farm, who lives in the City, and paid us a long visit there one day with Mr. B's little boy. So the eldest son, as we understand has been thrown into prison, and she, his mother, wanted A. to say that her son had nothing to do with it. But how could he, much though he longed to do so for we don't believe it for a moment, and we liked him so much.

So now it seems there is the married daughter, almost blind with Opthalmia, from working my bag, and the eldest son in prison through us too.

The head of the Twansheo (Elders of the District) also interviewed A. The man, who came out and gesticulated so yesterday, was not a Yamen runner, but the Head of the Family, who came out to tell the news. It is considered very serious.

A quite poor woman has died at a cottage in the valley beneath us, and at night it was pretty to see lights all along the curving path for a considerable distance. People here said they were bonfires of paper, whether paper Cash I do not know. Unfortunately now there are Taoist rites all night long, the music is not ugly at a distance, and to my ear rather cheery, but the dogs, keep being awakened by each fresh outburst and barking. And one wishes the poor woman could have had more fuss made about her in her life time instead of so much now.

In companies of 4 and 5, men are digging up all the ground round, so I suppose some fresh crop is going in, more important than Turnips, which have so far seemed generally planted at once, wherever another crop was taken up. The Hedge of Tea Bushes behind the Farm is coming into fine flower now, and the white Hibiscus lovely. I went out before breakfast again, and gathered what seemed the last of the red Guernsey Lilies. I also got some Gold and Silver Honeysuckle and found two kinds of Ferns and a very pretty Moss, like what I discovered—till then unknown—near I-chang, all growing together. There seemed to be quite a new Flora in the prettily broken up rocky bit of ground where the Lilies were growing in such profusion, Weather quite lovely again now although sun rather too hot yesterday.

September 22nd. Great piece of work at the grand house at which the Missionaries have rooms, making cakes for the festival on the 15th of the Chinese Moon. Two men with Mallets four feet long, made out of whole Locust trees, were using them as pestles: one disengaging the sticky Glutinous rice off the others Mallet by a dexterous blow. Four of the good lady's Tenants had come in to officiate, and a great assemblage was looking on with much fun and merriment, reminding us of the stirring of our Christmas puddings. Later on the cakes were borne in triumph by a bevy of men, and patted and flattened out into about the size of Dinner plates. We had had some for Supper, and uncommonly stick-jaw we found them, but, I can fancy their being good eaten with Sugar water, when one is very hungry. At our farm there have been no merry doings. The Tall Millet was brought in the other day to be thrashed but gradually every one has abandoned the Farm. The stirring mistress has been for two days kneeling and weeping in A's office begging him to say her son had nothing to do with our Robbery. He lent her 10,000 Cash to mollify the Runners hearts, that her son might not be put into an instrument of Torture, that seems to answer to the Maiden of our Middle Ages, and said if she could get the Head of the Twenty Elders of the District, who must have known him always, to testify to his character, he would send in this testimony to the Consul, and ask him to do what can be done. To-day the poor young man's very dirty hard worked drudge of a wife—What a thing it is to be a Daughter in Law in China! has gone into town too and the Farmer himself appears no more, so now there are only the three Children, bright faced, little Hae Ching, who is at School all day, and his younger brother of the horrible Skin Disease, who was again crying himself to sleep the other night—but it seems they will not send him into the Hospital to be cured, though Dr. D. says the only hope of doing so, is to have him under treatment, and quite still for a fortnight.—And then there is the small brother. Beside these three boys, there are now only the other Lodgers, and ourselves. We have alarms of thieves every night, the dogs bark furiously keeping everyone from sleeping, and there really was a robbery the night before last at the neighbouring village.

To-day A. unable any longer to bear the thought of the misery, we have any how been the means of bringing upon these poor people, has written to the Consul asking if he can find out, whether what we have heard is true, and asking him if so to tell the Magistrate, that while of course not presuming to interfere with Chinese justice, yet if it be but a question of recovering the stolen goods he would rather renounce them for ever, than bring such trouble on our Hosts. The last time the Farmer appeared however he rather puzzled us. It was two nights ago in the evening, and I remarked at once he had been drinking wine, he was so jovial. A. could not believe it, because he said he had been dining at the Tu Shan Temple. But on enquiry it appeared that he had had both wine and meat there. "At a Buddhist Temple?" persisted A. "Why yes!" said the Farmer. "You see it is the festival of a very bad Pusa (or Image). "What do you worship a bad Pusa for!" "Why! we must! He is the head of all the Wolves, and night Depredators." Then there followed a talk about the Monastery we stayed at on Mount Omi, and that at the Hoa Ngai, where neither wine nor meat were allowed, and there were no bad Pusa, our Hu-peh Cook interrupting with much warmth. to ask "Did we not know the Temple at Wuchang, the capital of his Province, on the back of the Tortoise Hill, which was in connexion with the Hoa Ngai, and where there were also no bad Pusa?" Then the Farmer went on to say "If you want to build, on a piece of my land here at the back among the Fir trees, it is beautifully cool there, and I should be glad to oblige you, you are such a kind man, and so good." "Shall you

Entrance to Hoa Ngai Monastery.

be here to-morrow?" asked A. "No, the day after" "Well, the day after I will go and have a look at it with you." He was stripped to the waist, as if it were the height of Summer to cool down after his wine drinking. There was not a word said about his eldest son in prison, nor about all the family trouble and disgrace. He has not appeared again since. And we do not know quite what to make of the little scene. As A. says: "The time to be on your guard is when a

Chinaman flatters you." It seemed an odd time to choose. The pigeons have two little ones, a great delight to the eldest boy, who is for ever clapping his hands to make his pigeons rise or come, making a sort of Æolian music through the air with the whistle fastened on to the Cock's tail. which gives forth one prolonged musical note more or less acute as his flight is faster or the reverse. The little Poney's ancle swelled again after our expedition on Sunday, so we have been bandaging it with cold water, tying it up again in one of my long, blue Sandal cloths. The little creature seems quite to understand it, and holds up his foot to be tied up, but does not approve of having his leg handled. The weather has turned very hot and oppressive again. A. says in the City yesterday it was well up on the nineties and he thought the hottest day this Summer. In the evening the clouds gathered round these hills, and we every minute expected a Thunder storm. But it passed off, and there was a lovely moonlight night again with only more wind than usual. Every where about the country they are burning the ground, mixing dried grass with the earth to keep it smouldering on. We sat by one of these fires at the nearest Gap in our hills last night enjoying the smell of the burning weeds, as well as the breeze and the moon-lit expanse before us. But the Summer is lasting very long this year, as great heat began before the middle of April. People, who have lived here some years, say however it is the coolest Summer they have known here.

September 23rd. The Farmer's wife came back last night, looking very sad; the Daughter in law, who had only been away all day, also returned. Bright faced, little Hae Ching now sits under the Walnut tree crying, the tears silently rolling down his cheeks at the thought of his brother's disgrace. They say he has been bambooed in the Yamen; also, we hear, put upon the rack. Our cook is begging us to cross the River at once, for he says there will be trouble on the country side, when this becomes known, I wonder if it has any connection with this, that the Coolie we sent across River with a note did not return but sent a substitute, and that the Boy has not come back. But this may simply be on account of the Feast on Sunday. All the Elders of the District are invited to dinner to-morrow, and A. wrote another letter to the Consul, but decided not to go in, so as to be present at the Dinner here, and say he has done what he could to get the eldest son off. We feel too sad to talk over things even now. This morning black mist over Chungking, a dull overcast day, and of course cooler. A. and I have been practising with Revolvers. The Elders are going by to dinner. Every thing seems sad,. such a contrast from the brilliant, sunshiny day, on which we gave our grand dinner on arrival. We had meant to give another, but just as we were about to send out invitations our Landlord's son was thrown into prison, and we felt it inexpedient.

September 24th. Another dull day with mist on all the mountain tops, but not such a black heavy cloud as yesterday. After long, long waiting probably because it was one of the three great Settling Days of the Chinese year, the dinner came off. The Elders were all most polite to A. said they knew he was a very good man, and that it was no fault of his. They brought a paper, which they were all signing, to testify to the goodness of the family on both sides, father's and mother's. Both families had been settled here for 150 years and were well known. On the other hand the Weaver was a very bad cearacter; known to be so, whom the Farmer's wife had only engaged out of compassion for his mother, a widow living in the valley below, who had two sons, and unfortunately both bad. Our cook after the dinner, at which he seemed to be hugely enjoying himself, when A. left, asked leave to go across the River to testify that the Eldest Son was not over here at the time of the Robbery. The Farmer's wife was serving at the dinner weeping before each Elder in turn. The Farmer himself, although an Eider was not able to be present. The married daughter, whose eyesight has gone, was here beforehand, with her poor, sore, running eyes, weeping and kneeling :

"Release my brother." A. could only say he had written a second time to the Consul to tell the Magistrate, he would rather give up all claim to his things than bring trouble on the family. But that it was not in his power to release him, nor even to go direct to the Magistrate to ask him to do so. We fear the Consul will not be at all willing to interfere in the matter. He certainly can not like doing so.

Meanwhile I cannot think what is happening to the crops. But the smells made by disturbing the Manure heaps, and carrying them by, are dreadful.

Went for a ride in the afternoon, and while sitting on a hill top reading the disputes over the Home Rule Bill the two coolies thought it very pleasant to sit on another, and as the little poney had been rolling about on a bank of Bracken with his saddle on, they took the saddle and brible and bells off. Tarchendo then rolled to his hearts content, at which we all laughed. After that he grazed contentedly for a while, till the idea seemed to enter his head at last that he was loose, and might as well go home. Off he went and as soon as he got into the path he set off cantering, and I expected to see him no more, till I should find him tied to his habitual tree. The old man evidently with the same idea laded himself with saddle and bells to carry home, but at the very steep turn of the road the soldier coolie caught him and brought him back, delighted to be of use once more. Met a great flock of ducks—about a thousand—waddling along the road in three detachments on the way home. Persimmons in season now, and Pears lasting on. As a rule fruits seem only to be in season for one week in Chungking. We have also had Chestnuts three times now, and little green Oranges are being handed about, which our boy says are "all the same Lemons." Their skin has a delicious fragrance.

September 25th. Where the Indian Corn and Tall Millet waved, when we arrived three months ago, now all the ground has been dug up to receive the Poppy Seed. They are but waiting for the rain to fall to put it in. Each day looks more threatening than the last, and each night a little rain falls as if the heavy black Sponge above us were squeezed by an invisible hand, but so far the rain holds off. This time last year we were floating down the Rapids of the River from Kiating in rain every day. It must come soon, and we only regret Chungking has not been washed out

Opinm Poppies.

before we go into it. People have had the Thermometer 97 in their rooms more than once this last week, and say it has been the most trying of all the Summer.

Nothing could be done for Hae Ching's brother yesterday because of the festival; but there was no one here to do reverence before the Ancestors tablets, and I do not know what has become of all the letters little Hae Ching was directing instead of his brother in prison this time. But I went to see the D's in the afternoon, and found their table all spread for dinner, two Incense sticks burning in the Censer. The eldest son of their house came in and reverenced, and in this case raised each pair of Joss sticks to a level with his eyes, which I had not seen done before. Then the feast was carried off to some back precincts to be eaten. It was a little distressing presently to see all the young men and even boys coming away with such very swollen flushed faces and watery eyes telling plainly of the strong drinks of which they had partaken. And when walking through the village this seemed pretty general. "All the same your Christmas time" a Chinaman would say, however.

Our Coolies wanted to know yesterday whether we wanted them to come in and salute us in the proper Chinese fashion at this Season, and were we also going to present them with 500 cash a piece. The way the two questions were put together was highly comic. After a little consultation we decided upon 1000 cash or 3s. between the three, and I said they certainly ought to salute us according to the Chinese etiquette. So they came in and knocked their foreheads on the floor. The Boy, who has been trained in "barbarian" Shanghai, could not of course think of doing such a thing.

October 6th. The Business house has been moving into new Premises. On the day it moved a fire was piled up high in our largest Charcoal Pan. This was tied between two bamboo poles, the fire lit, and then carried through the streets like a Sedan chair. I am told when a house is bought the principal beam is taken out of the roof, and a new one put in, lest the new owner should be held responsible for any debts contracted by the former possessor, and the like. In the evening the scene was very pretty. In the new house there is Courtyard beyond Courtyard, and there were innumerable Chinese Lanterns and Lamps hanging, and pots full of flowers: the

Dinner Party with Theatricals.

chairs all covered with red cloth embroideries, a red rug on the floor in the end room of all, and deep red Kakemonos hanging all round on the walls, presented for the occasion. Everyone connected with the Hong was in full Mandarin dress, high boots, long satin over coat reaching to the boots, official cap with red tassel. They all came and bowed before A., very solemnly stretching their clasped hands down to their kness then raising them quickly up to their mouths. To my surprise they came into the inner Private Office, into which I had retired and had the politeness to repeat the same ceremony before me. There were Artistes from the various Theatres singing in their peculiar fashion, once or twice rather agreeably I thought, but often in what sounded like a series of harsh and yet harsher groans, oftenest of course in their favourite high falsetto. And there were many guests, all of whom sat down to a supper at little tables scattered about. That was on the 29th September. Now for four days there is a dinner and theatrical Performance going on at the Hunan and Hupeh Guild, the finest in the city. Yesterday about 90 sat down to dinner, and I fancy there were all the principal merchants there; the Head of the Eight guilds, a venerable man with a white beard, said to be 89 but looking in very good case of 72, sat in the place of honour. People were invited for one or two, but I think the guests hardly arrived before 4, all in Official dress. The dinner was about 6, and one of the most interesting sights was to see one of the Head men in the business go round to each guest in turn, bowing solemnly in afore mentioned manner, which the guest returned in like style, and then conducting him at least part of the way to his assigned table, pausing in going to poour out a glass of wine, and offer it, also the Chop sticks. Before that began he poured out two libations, one before and one behind,. and at the same time there was a great explosion of crackers, and a sort of tom-toming. Slow music was played, and the actors, who took female parts, now came round in red robes to pour wine for the guests. Meanwhile all the guests and people of the Hong stood in a crowd at either side watching. Till then they had sat at little tables, sipping tea and smoking, till the light refreshment before dinner came in the shape of two dumplings stuffed with forced meat and two stuffed with sweets, also a bowl of soup. The entrance of the more distinguished guests was also rather amusing, for they went round to table after table making the ceremonious bow and smiling all over.

Stage with Actors.

I sat in a side box with screens all round, the wife and children of the Head man keeping me company. It was amusing to see her intense delight, when she saw her husband conducting the people to their seats. She had five jackets on, and a pretty tea green silk over skirt. She and her boys were very lively, the youngest, only 4, was always inviting me to drink wine with him in the most solemn manner. The native wine is very mild, and the cups very small, but I fancy this very precocious child would be better without it. The Actors both days displayed a board with the 5 Happinesses upon it, turned in my direction, directly I appeared, although I was supposed not to be seen. They came and asked A. which play they should act—they had an enormous ivory Tusk covered with names. He chose one, and they put it on at once. Of course there is no scenery. But there is a great variety of fine clothes. And what memories they must have to know so many pieces so well as to need no preparation! The populace stood below in the Courtyard, enjoying the spectacle for nothing, and very much they seemed to do so. One man had brought his basket in, and stood it in front of him. Suddenly there was he tearing after another man, who was attempting to run off with it! No one else moved in the crowd, they were all absorbed in the Play. The opening piece yesterday was supposed to be appropriate to the occasion, about a Fishermen so kind he would only fish with straight hooks. If the fish were fated to be killed he would catch them, not otherwise. So the Emperor distinguished him, and raised him to high place and he surrounded the throne with good men and true.

To-day the piece was laughable. The audience mosty dealt in Drugs. Meanwhile the poor eldest son of the Farm never gets out of prison. His mother comes again and again, and yesterday got another 10,000 Cash lent her, and to-day our Cook was ever so long at the magistrate's Yamen, but it seems some one must go Bail and the person willing to do that has not yet been found.

October 15th. Mr. R. was to bring his two little boys to breakfast at 8 o'clock this morning but though we waited half an hour we had long ago finished, when they appeared. Breakfast was brought back, but they also had long finished when a most elegant apparition came courtesying through the Courtyard, their elder sister of 13, a really very pretty girl in her to-day's toilette with bright brown eyes, and a graceful, alert step, in spite of tiniest feet. But then the young woman was rouged, and powdered, and her lips coloured; all her hair in a twist on the top of her head stuck all over with very pretty pins, made of imitation pearls and blue Jay's feathers, with a cap (or bonnet) all round it, Jay's wings and jewels

Child Visitors.

ornamenting this, gold pins fastening her hair at the back, three bandeaux of artificial flowers round her forehead, whirls of them at the side and a very pretty disposition of them down the back of her head and neck. She wore a lovely rose brocade over jacket with black satin collar, a mauve under jacket, which did not show, and trowsers of a rather richer rose, all embroidered too. Her little sister of six was only a little less elegantly dressed, and looked like the most charming doll, when I made her lie back in one of our chairs covered with a goat skin rug, and play at going to sleep. The youngest brother, who is evidently the pride of the family, had the same criarde combination of colours as usual, rose coloured satin hat, purple coat, red trowsers, and his hair cut short like a priest's. At last the little girls went away after I had twice photo'd them but the little boys were still hanging on, when at 12-30 we started to cross the river. If they ever came to an end, Chinese visits would not be so trying.

A few mornings ago A. was surprised by a visit from two gentlemen, whilst we sat at breakfast. One was Number Four Young Master of the Yuen family, our country neighbours, the other an Ex-Official, just returned from Peking. It seemed they actually wished to see me, so they were brought up stairs. And the Ex-Official after a little while said it would be so nice, if I would give his sons instruction in English. I asked what age they were. It seemed there were two, 12 and 14. I laughingly said "Perhaps they would be afraid of me." "Oh no!" Finally I agreed, thinking as we were soon going away, that would break it off if tiresome. To my horror I found then, that he proposed that they should come and live in our house, as his home was out by the Hoa Ngai Monastery, where we stayed last year, about a day's journey from here. I said "Perhaps they would get into mischief—English boys would! Perhaps they would break things." The father a nice mannered man with a very grave, gentle face, seemed greatly shocked at this idea. But he said, if I liked, he would take a room for them in an Inn, and send them here each day for an hour to learn English. They must be pursuing their Chinese studies all day long and could not consequently get into any mischief. With this he went away, and so far I have heard no more about my two young men, whom I was apparently to teach for the pleasure of doing so. A. however really has undertaken Mr. S's nice, elder son, who is to make himself useful in his Office—**if** he can. The little fellow of 5, who never speaks, is actually said already to know 2,000 Chinese characters. It is terrible to think of.

I went over to see the new Hong by day light the other day. They could not pay me much attention, because taking me over it, someone's eye was caught by a door opening on to an outside Porch, commanding a fine view all over the river. The door from this to the house was right in the middle of it, and of the house; thus, as they said, affording most easy access to the Demons. And every one was full of suggestions as to what should be done, for obviously no one could expect to make money in a house with demons walking straight in, whenever they liked. I recommended a leaf shaped door, as so particularly curly-whirly but was evidently considered frivolous. So I went on to see the part of the house we may eventually occupy. It is inhabited now by four Chinese families **such** a number of women, so dirty and draggled looking; one, the principal one, with a big wen upon her forehead. But anything to equal the magnificence of the carved and gilded bedsteads I never did see! they have a raised ledge at the side, very convenient to lay the quilt on, when out of use or any extra coverings. At the other side, that towards the room, are two seats, one at the bed head, one at the foot. On these the Chinese sit whilst dressing and undressing, laying their clothing mostly on the bed as extra covering. All two sides of the room were lined with cupboards, highly black lacquered with black drop handles. Seats without backs were placed against these, all the length of them; there seemed no place for doing anything. And every thing except the furniture looked so squalid and dilapidated I do not know how we ever can live there. But the Hong says the house could be done up for a small outlay, and has a little garden, an immense advantage.

View of Our Mountain as seen from Chungking.

The Hong, greatly to my surprise, has set its heart on my staying here when A. has to go down river, keeping the seals, and the money, and generally managing the business. They seem to think this quite natural, and what a Chinese lady would do.

* * * * *

Nikko, Japan, August 3rd 1894. Thus abruptly and somewhat sorrowfully my Farm Diary, begun with such a light heart, came to an end. Perhaps it was blood poisoning from all those dreadful smells — the Doctor said it was — perhaps it was grief over the distress we had brought on others, it well might have been! anyhow I wrote no more. And yet, even in China things come right in the end sometimes. One day a most wretched looking, emaciated, red eyed, disfigured creature threw himself in the dust before me, and knocked his head repeatedly. I rather hurried away from him because there were the Farmer and his wife, asking A. to sit down and drink wine with them to celebrate the release of their son from Prison, and I wanted to congratulate them, and ask how he was; then with a sudden horror realised that the wretched creature, who had just knelt before me, had once been the strong, hearty man, who used always to call out in such loud, cheery tones: "Is it cool enough for you, **T'ai t'ai?**" on his frequent visits to his parents home. We felt then we could not take part in the feast of congratulation. But he is a Chinaman. And since then he seems quite to have got over his Torturing in the Yamen. Our things have been recovered, the Thieves have been exhibited in four cages outside the Farm house, and the honour of the Farm family is intact once more. Our big brute of a Coolie disappeared without his wages one day. He was the most powerful man I have come across in these parts. But he had stolen someone's jacket. And though it was recovered, he returned no more. Our Cook has married a Szechuan woman after all in spite of all his wise saws, the Farmer's wife playing the part of Middle woman. A new building site has been given us, nearly as good as the old, and thus ends all likelihood of our ever again living in a Szechuan Farm house, the homely details of whose doings may however have some interest for those who like to realise that great Division of the Human Race, called Chinese, consists not only of China-men but of real men and women, with simple wants and wishes not after all so unlike our own.

Roots of Hoang Ko Tree.

Lightning Source UK Ltd.
Milton Keynes UK
UKHW031251060521
383231UK00004B/236